JOHN THOMPSON'S

FIRST NURSERY RHYMES

T0084941

12105

Teachers and Parents

This collection of favorite nursery rhymes, written in the John Thompson tradition, is intended as supplementary material for beginning and early elementary level pianists. The pieces may also be used by more advanced students for sight-reading practice. The material is not specifically graded, although pieces appearing later in the book tend to be more demanding than the earlier ones. Dynamics, phrasing and tempo indications have been deliberately omitted, since initially the student's attention should be focused on playing notes and rhythms accurately. Outline fingering has been included, and in general the hand is assumed to remain in a five-finger position until a new fingering indicates a position shift. The fingering should suit most hands, although logical alternatives are always possible.

The Willis Music Company
Florence, Kentucky 41022-0548

Illustrations by xheight Limited

12105

WILLIS MUSIC

Pease Porridge Hot

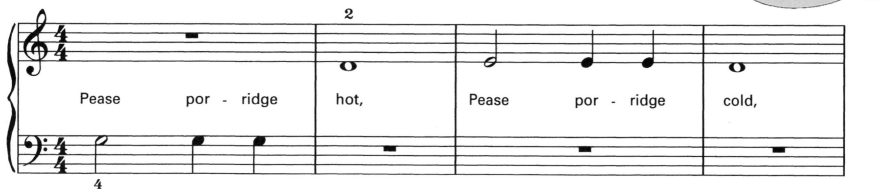

Pease por - ridge hot, Pease por - ridge cold,

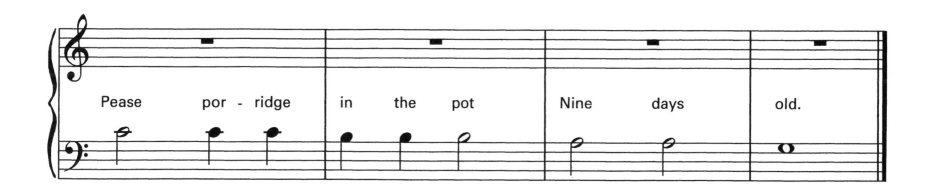

Pease por - ridge in the pot Nine days old.

Cobbler, Cobbler

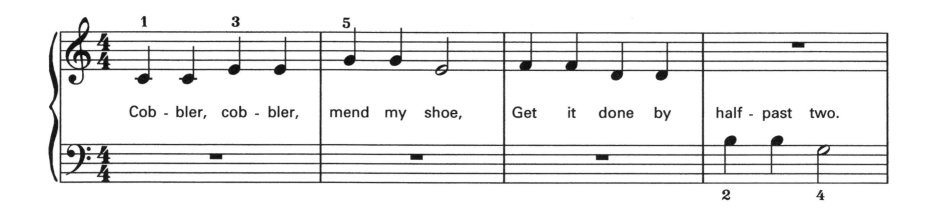

Cob - bler, cob - bler, | mend my shoe, | Get it done by | half - past two.

My toe is | peep - ing through, | Cob - bler, cob - bler, | mend my shoe.

Mary, Mary, Quite Contrary

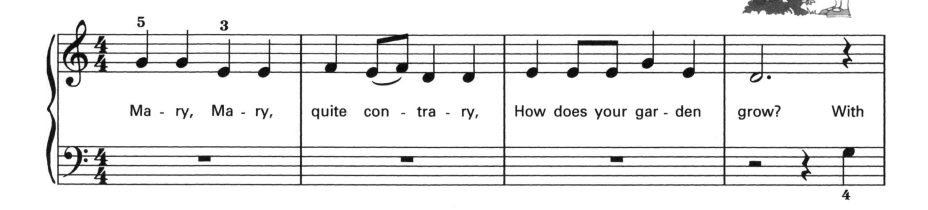

Ma - ry, Ma - ry, quite con - tra - ry, How does your gar - den grow? With

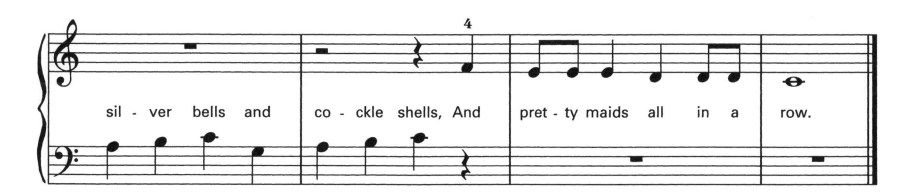

sil - ver bells and co - ckle shells, And pret - ty maids all in a row.

Diddle, Diddle,Dumpling, My Son John

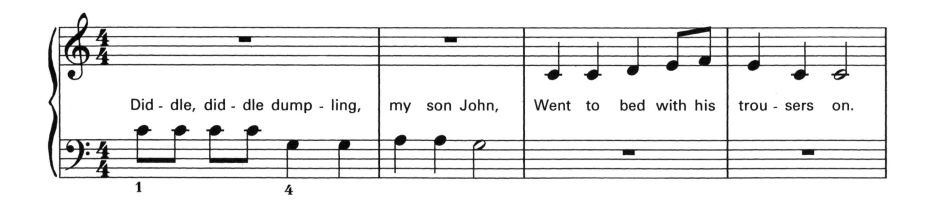

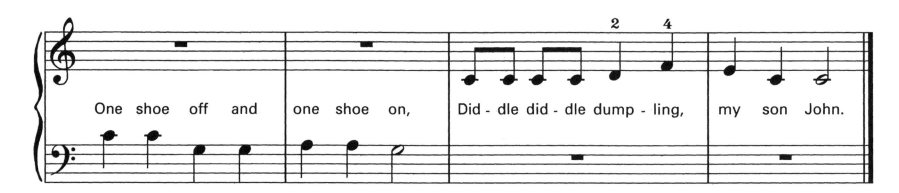

Bobby Shaftoe

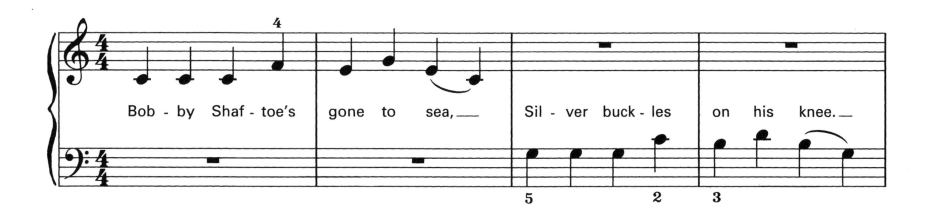

Bob - by Shaf - toe's gone to sea, ___ Sil - ver buck - les on his knee. ___

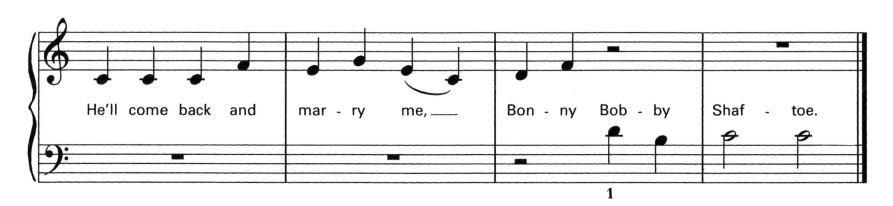

He'll come back and mar - ry me, ___ Bon - ny Bob - by Shaf - toe.

Hickory Dickory Dock

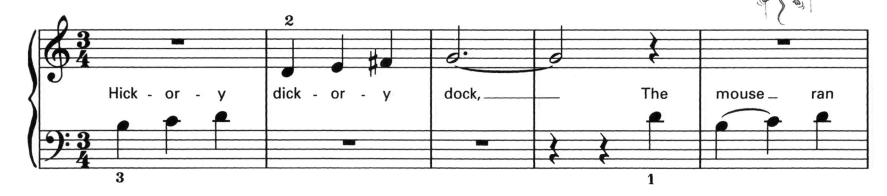

Hick - or - y dick - or - y dock, _____ The mouse _ ran

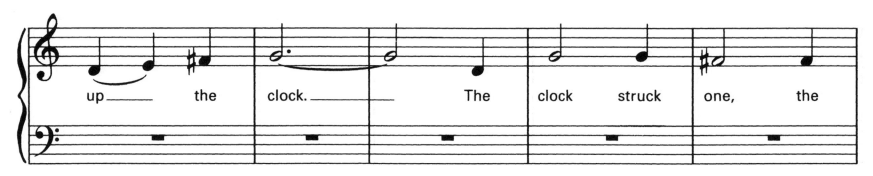

up _____ the clock. _____ The clock struck one, the

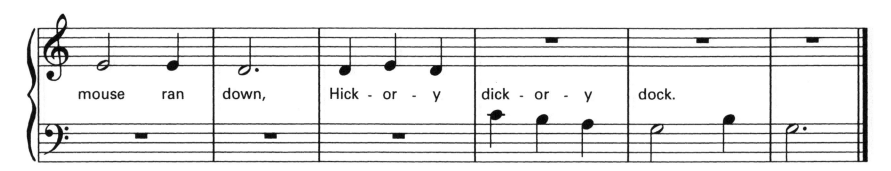

mouse ran down, Hick - or - y dick - or - y dock.

Jelly on the Plate

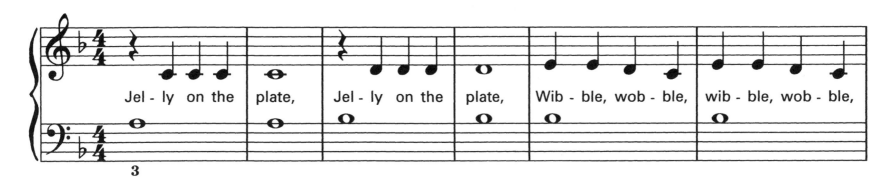

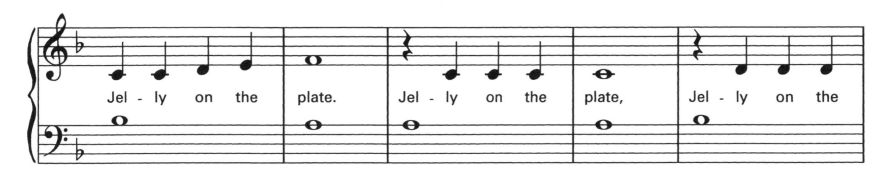

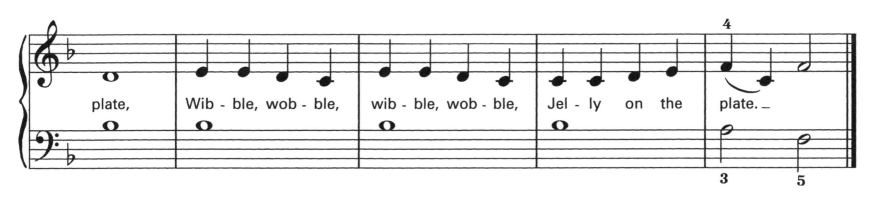

Little Boy Blue

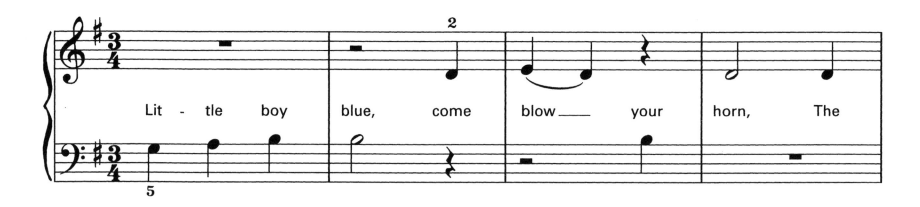

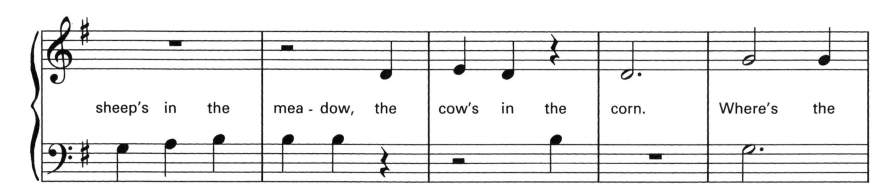

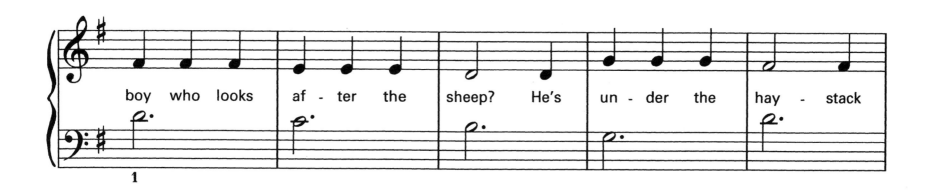

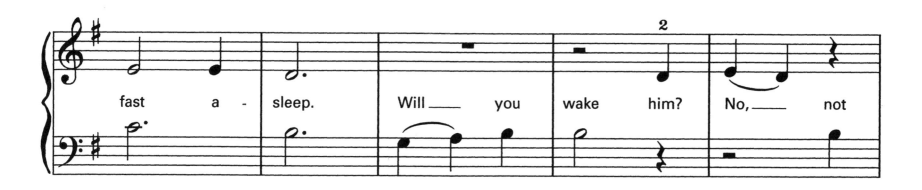

Girls and Boys Come Out to Play

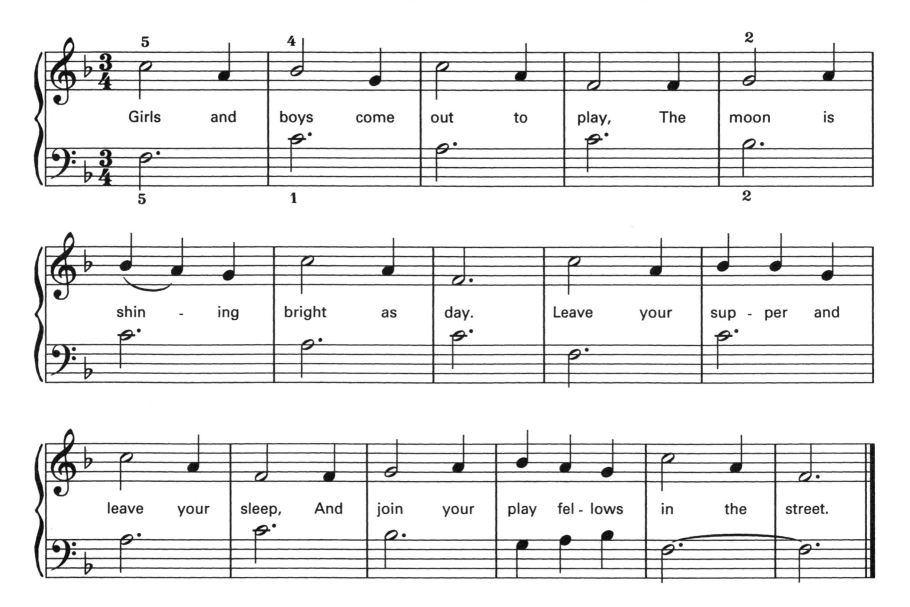

One Man Went to Mow

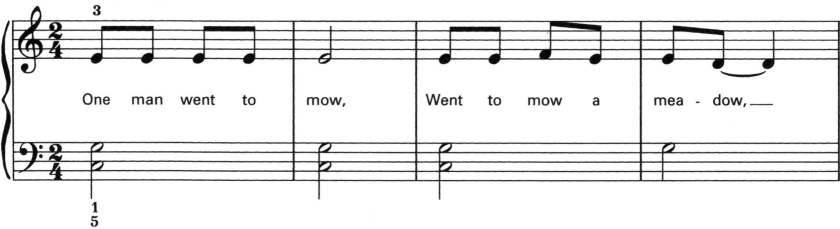

One man went to mow, Went to mow a mea - dow, ___

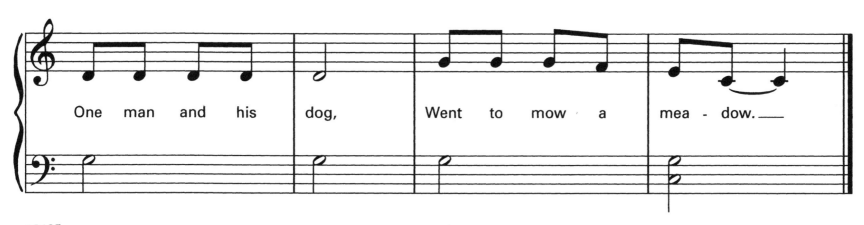

One man and his dog, Went to mow a mea - dow. ___

12105

The Grand Old Duke of York

Little Miss Muffet

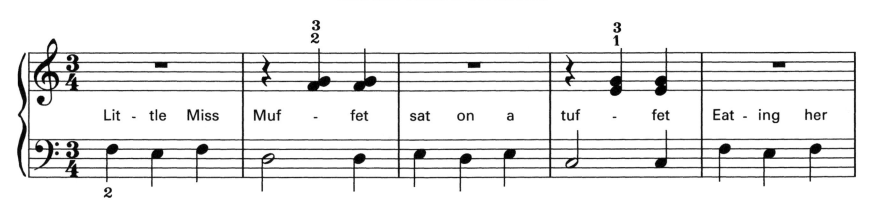

Lit - tle Miss Muf - fet sat on a tuf - fet Eat - ing her

curds and whey. There came a big spi - der who

sat down be - side her And fright - ened Miss Muf - fet a - way.

Oranges and Lemons

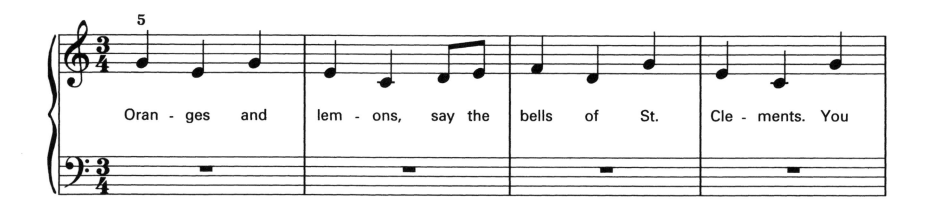

12105

There Was a Princess Long Ago

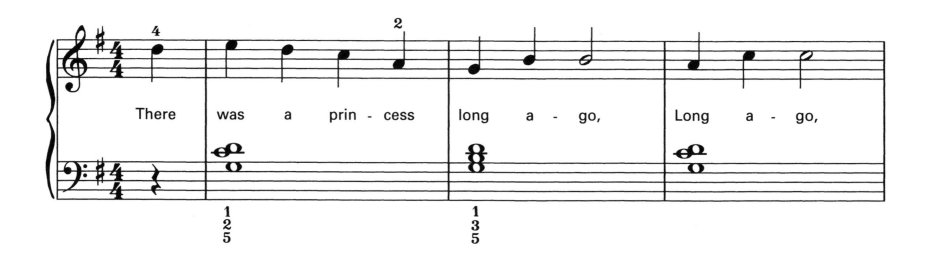

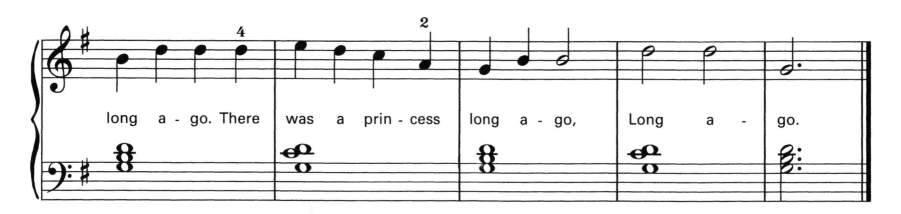

The Barnyard Song

20

Incy Wincy Spider

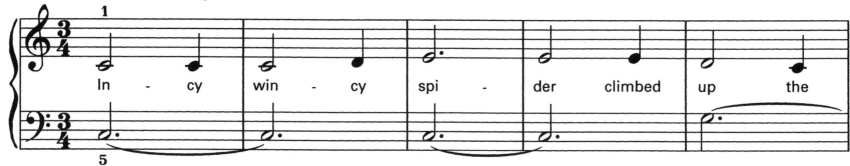

In - cy win - cy spi - der climbed up the

wa - ter spout, _____

12105

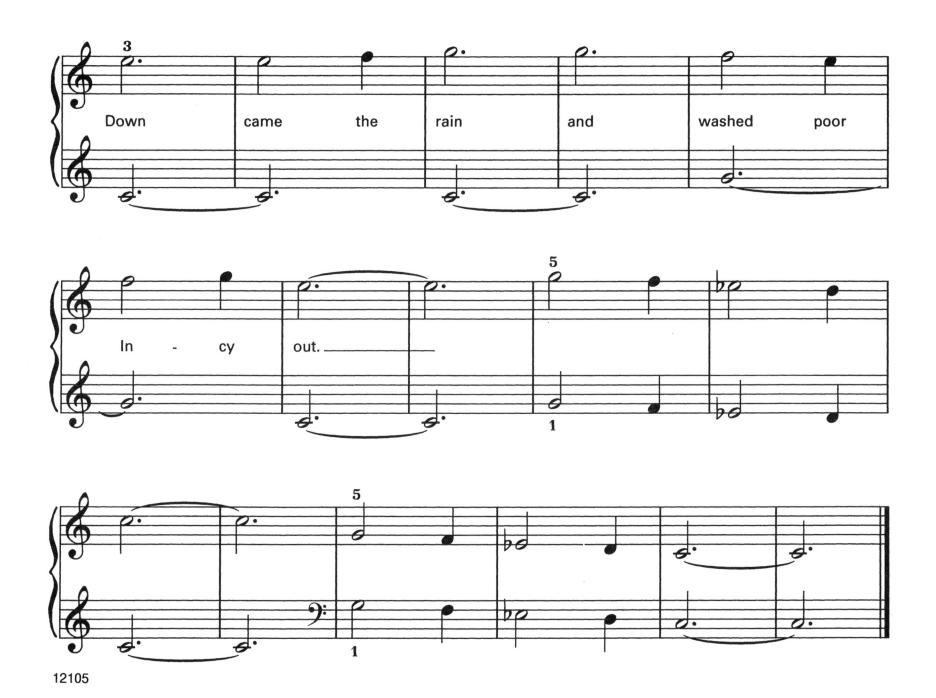

Ding Dong Bell

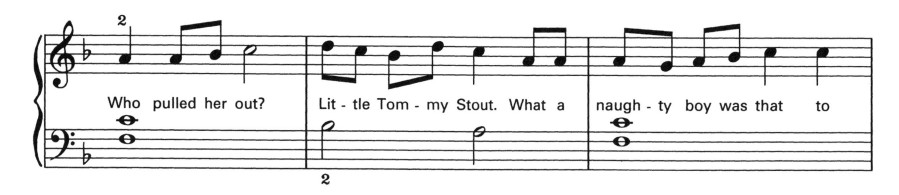

Trot, Trot, Trot

Hush-a-by Baby

Little Arabella Miller

Moderato

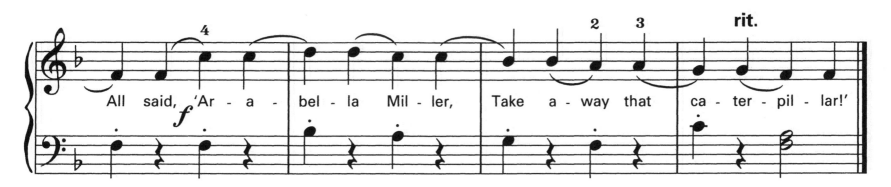

Seagull, Seagull

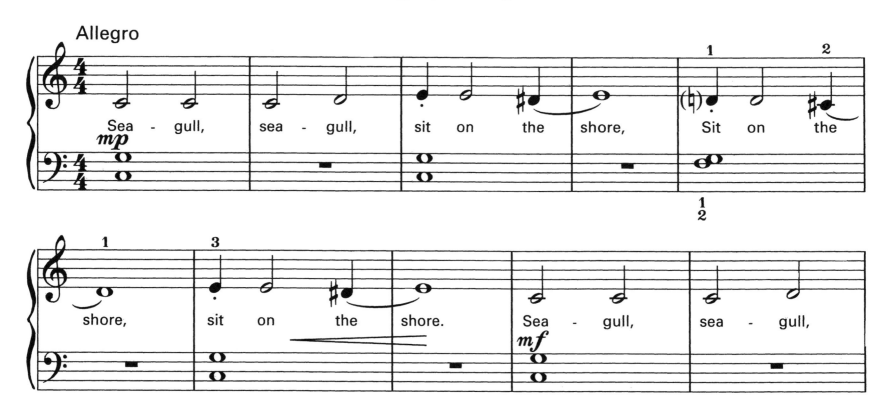

Oh, We Can Play on the Big Bass Drum

Tambourine, Tambourine

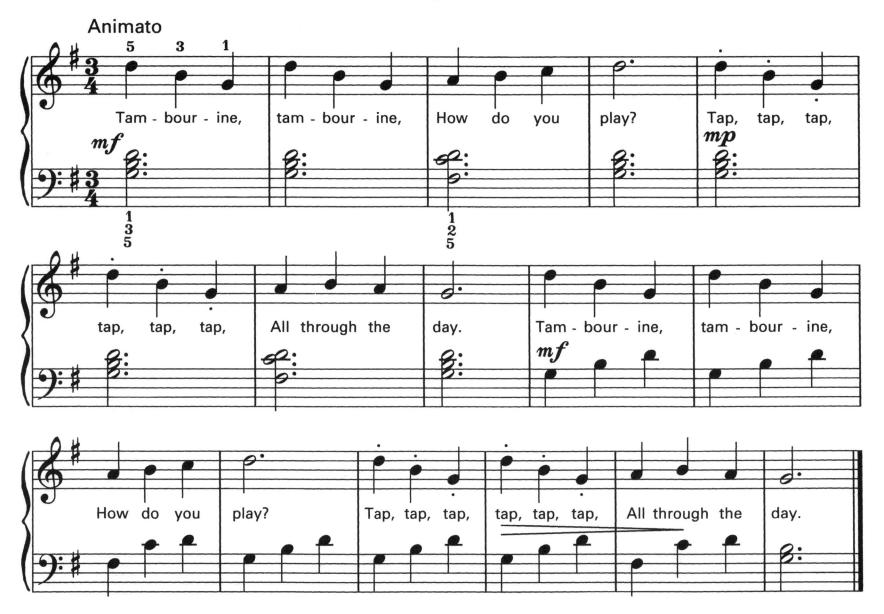

Georgie Porgie

Three Little Kittens

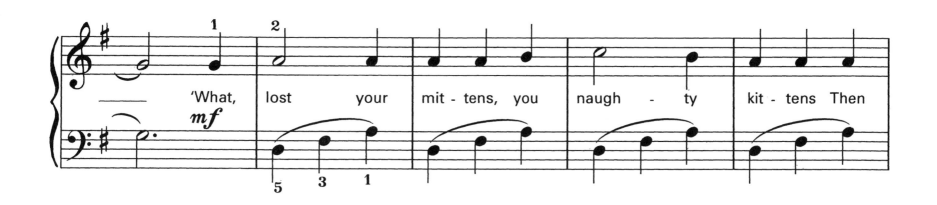

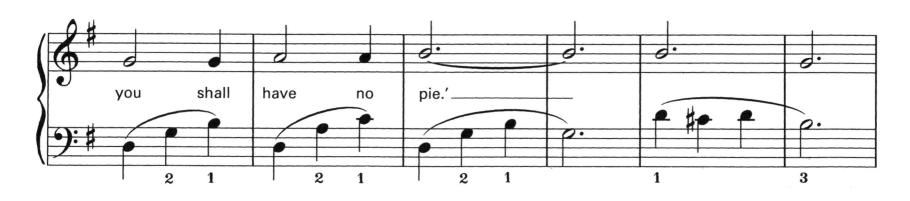

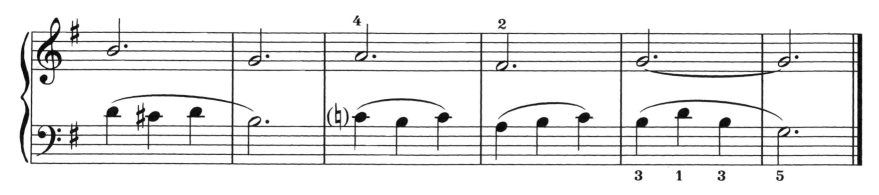

Ladybird, Ladybird

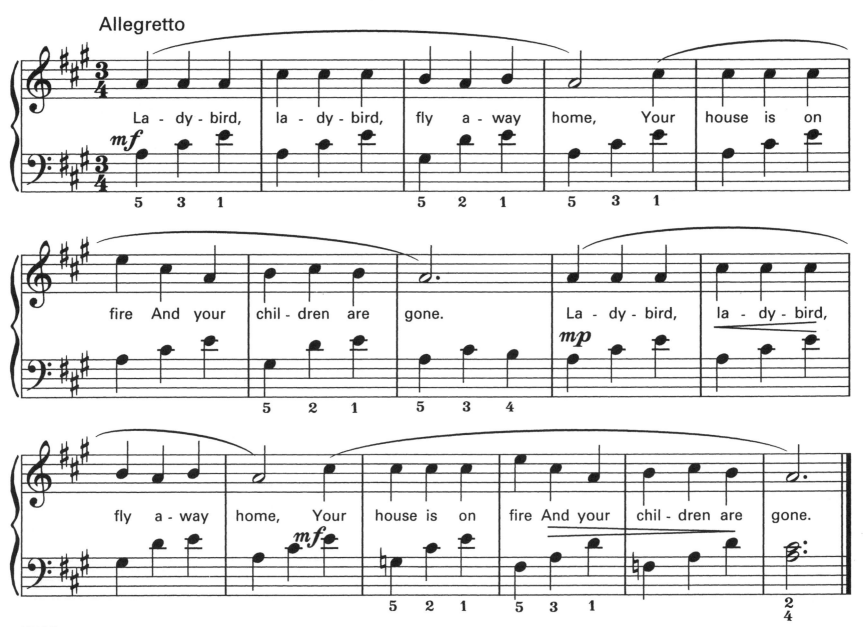